ZEN DAYS, ZEN NIGHTS

Other books by Solee MacIsaac
Joy Shared
A Beloved Speck in the Universe
Little Wisdoms

Zen Days, Zen Nights

Solee MacIsaac

EVERY BOOK PRESS
MMXXIII

© Copyright 2023 Solee MacIsaac
All rights reserved.
ISBN: 978-0-9837714-7-0

Cover Photo:
Solee MacIsaac
Book Design:
William Bentley

INTRODUCTION

There isn't time to read an essay, or plan an in-depth study. There isn't time to read many lines. Zen days, Zen nights are here. Hold your head at a slight angle, don't think too much, rest in your insight. Small points of interest can ignite a roaring flame, sending sparks to Heaven. If you will, read with compassion.

Solee MacIsaac

These Zen-like haiku phrases are dedicated to my first born, beautiful woman, and mother herself, Michele. She taught herself to read when only 6 years old, and has never stopped reading since.

March of days,
Leads the trail of nights
To the edge of Zen.

ZEN DAYS, ZEN NIGHTS

Silence
Is the company
Of my thoughts.

White and fragile
The closed
Night blossoms.

Stretching across my bed
Moonlight
Sleeps.

Brown and gray dusk
Breeds hopes and dreads,
Watching crows feed.

Every ounce
Of precious wine,
Secures a tranquil rest.

Great symphonies
Crash through
My open night window.

Let all beings rest silent
Next to their
Dreams.

Sadness trails
Willow branches
Through the dark pond.

Oak trees whispering
Gossip,
Leaving daylight behind.

Generous
The green cushion of blades
For my swollen feet.

Hours before the light returns
Soft-padded steps
Sound loud.

Stones, small fishes, grass,
All indistinguishable
Until dawn.

Why cry out —
The dark swallows
All unnecessary sound.

Many hopes hinged
On breaking day,
Dashed in morning's glare.

Sweet sleep
Dancing in the blown
White curtain.

Leaves drifting
On first shaft
Of Autumn morn.

Rubbing my eyes,
Straining between
Light and shadow.

What is real?
Love and light? Rest and dark?
Me and my Self?

Tiptoeing lightly,
Opening blinds,
To new possibilities.

Cats sleep,
Except for
Their whiskers.

How quiet
Deep night
Becomes.

Keep an open hearth,
Weary travelers
Arrive cold and hungry.

Night shields
Blemished beauty.
The Moon has its flaws.

Reflected radiance
Is light from another
Love.

Dip your pen
In the inky dark,
Paint the light with nothing.

The eyeball inside is dark,
Outside light has no obstacle
To the brain.

The instant you see you,
Don't look
Away.

An empty mind
Is clear
Of trouble.

Evening passes
Quickly,
Night must have her reign.

Night visions
Do not require
Eyes.

What depths
Are revealed
In Love's eyes.

The long road to dawn
Travels through
Dark country.

Blink, blink,
Too much light
Spoils tender roots.

Chocolate dreams,
Smooth and creamy,
Deep rich rest.

Stretched
Shadows race
To catch me.

Into the dark
With wide eyes
Streaming.

Cresting the night,
Sun's rays piercing
Treetops.

Light painting white
All the dark grays
Of night.

Petals opening,
Birds chirping,
Honoring new morning.

Lighting lightest light,
Sky of milk
Whitening all.

Alone in the dawn
Watching the
Pink cloudlets.

Sailing in the sunlight
My heart rides
In the wind boat.

Light has no shadow
To accompany
The journey.

Upside down
Parasols
Collect dew.

Gargoyles guard
Highest ramparts;
Grimace at sun shafts.

Day advances
With us
Or without us.

Night demons,
Day demons,
Hearts need champions.

Angels need not
Day or night,
To work or rest.

How far to go
Before love
Can soothe beating heart?

The day is long
Leading my steps
To eternity.

So much in a day
Can go right or wrong.
Who decides? Who judges?

Love follows me
In case I trip
And fall into it.

Don't be misled,
All is not lost,
Just waiting to be found.

Hidden in plain
Daylight
We seek You out.

Bound to the light,
Day describes
Our world of moments.

The first thought
Is never
The last.

Sunset hailing
Evening's approach
Blazes momentous glory.

Shortening into dusk
Light shatters into
Twilight.

Rotation complete
Earth does not stop
To admire or contemplate.

Throughout our
Motionless Universe
Movement erupts.

Moments, days,
Years, lifetimes;
Eternity's fractions.

Spirals of love
Secure all things
In proper position.

Our tender psyche
Knows so little
Of the wide omnipresence.

His face turned away,
Only the Moon and stars
Remember his day.

Feel into the dark
Dreaming night,
Your guide to the light.

Silk threads
Dress the night
In blackest velvet.

White gulls screaming
In the wind
Over the wild ocean.

Joy is my companion
Following the pathway
Home.

Clear focus
Occurs
Only in the Present.

The mask of night
Is pierced with
Enticing beacons.

Even in the day
The stars are shining
Just as brightly.

Night dream traces
Across our waking moments,
Contorting memories.

We are built on piles
Of colorful moments
With barely a tie to them all.

Flying
Is a matter
Of lightness.

Do the leaves
Confer
On when to fall?

In the dark,
Turning leaves are the same.
Day reveals brilliant differences.

Red, gold, fuchsia,
Sailing boatless
Past my window.

Night sounds
Magnify
Dark thoughts.

Is it lonely
Watching light change
Reflected in my eyes?

Dusk crawls slowly
Up the bedroom wall
Spilling over into night.

Trees shed
Summer garb
To sleep in the nude.

Mountain pines
Through wind moans
Learn valley gossip.

The Moon, like the Sun,
Is generous
With her light.

The dark isn't actually real,
But only a shadow
Punctuating light.

Knowing your Self
Avoids
Waste.

Pine needles soften
My walk,
Lightening my mood.

Autumn sunlight
Glancing off
Tired leaves.

Ponds mimicking
Colorful world
That they are not.

Nothing is nearly
As alarming
As one's own thoughts.

Night phantasies
Claw at my horizons
With renewed fervor.

Some unresolved issues
Grow strong
In darkness.

Night is for deep rest,
Day for action,
In between is forever.

Alone
Is quiet and
Simple.

Raking in the
Multicolor tree gowns.
More tomorrow.

Taking a moment
To drink in
Outrageous beauty.

Nothing
Lasts forever,
Except You.

I want
Nothing more
Than You.

Careless of me
To lose
Sight of You.

Dangerously close, love, light,
You and me;
Then, only You.

Gold-dipped treetops
Waving scattered clouds
Together again.

Autumn skies
Flinging birds
Home.

Nature leads,
We follow until
We grow beyond ourselves.

Leaving nature behind
To become
Super-Natural.

Every flower knows
Every bee's
Desire.

Leaves fall to nourish
Dry ground,
Covering Winter's sleep.

Standing still
For just a moment
Of retrospection.

Sandwiched between
Outer and inner life,
I watch.

Our inner child
Delights
In the simple.

After morning rain
Sunlight sparkles
On ephemeral diamonds.

Noon shadows
Barely exist,
Grow with afternoon.

Moon peeking over hillside
Lighting
Silver torches.

Stealth so secured
In black wells of dark,
But for green glowing eyes.

Shoes crunching
Through Fall's treasures
On the pumpkin trail.

Ice cream dreams,
With whipped cream clouds,
And strawberry streams.

Dark creeps along the edges
Of things
Dulling our senses slowly.

Sleep, Dark's companion,
Follows unnoticed,
Unrecognized.

Weeping willow
Loosens her heavy leaves
Born away in the burbling stream.

Setting Sun burns away top layer
Of melted ocean,
Leaking gold to the shore.

Warm your hands
In the firelight,
Sleep comes upon us.

Dreams ride the night horses
Flying free
With no boundaries.

Morning ablutions
Revive daytime life
With renewed assertions.

Circulation of Earth's breath,
Our days and nights
Bring rich impressions.

Gray dawn,
Morning glory
Still closed.

Day accelerates,
Climbing Heaven's steps
One moment at a time.

Descending the sky-sea,
Heaven's shining ship
Sinks with an explosion of color.

Night sky is decorated
With star jewels,
Promising a rich tomorrow.

Night gathers herself
Into her blackest cloak,
And breathes dream tales.

The very long turn from the light
Travelled so far,
Became the dawn again.

Go the distance,
You won't get lost,
You will find your Self again.

Inside yourself
Reflect,
Let the child loose.

Refresh,
Life restores herself
With renewed vigor.

Winter's snow melts in Spring,
Evaporates in Summer,
Sinks deep in Fall.

We are not apart from Nature
But must go through it,
In order to transcend all.

Messages abound,
Look deeper,
Deciphering Love takes a lifetime.

Blue white morning
Layers light
Over every surface.

Touch the hem
Of Night's garment,
Swiftly swirl into dreams.

Dressed in day colors,
Awake to
Daydreams.

See, touch, hear
From the beginning place,
Discard complacency.

Resting simple,
Black Cat stretches
Into Night.

Fragrances in the dark
So filling
Compared to daytime whiffs.

Climbing roses
Where are you going?
"To God" they sing.

Laughter in the day, cheerful.
Laughter in the dark
Ominous.

We differ,
But not like Day and Night,
We are all shades of Dawn.

Pathway to heaven
Is lined with
Kneeling Angels.

Our star high in sky
Remains,
While we turn away again.

Solar flares,
Even the Sun
Has tribulations.

Why sleep
In full Daylight?
Night is long and dark.

Seeing in the dark
Is for cats and owls,
Our sight starts with inner vision.

Don't believe everything
You see, hear, feel, or think;
Trust is for higher levels.

Sleep can cure fatigue
But is an unfortunate
Daylight companion.

Reach for Daylight.
Too far?
Grow a longer arm.

The darkest hour
Precedes the first rays
Of brilliant dawn.

Good Days,
Bad Days,
Better than any night.

Walking in Daylight
Each step
Alive in my heart.

Sleep spreads a thick cloak
Over the harsh glare
Of too much truth.

My Day,
My Life…
Is it, though?

Crystallized light
Dripping from frozen branches
In Spring Morning rays.

If you had to design a school
For humans to learn virtues,
Would it be this?

If the moment is all there is,
Shrink your Self
Into the Now.

A flower opens,
An eye opens:
Light.

From tall treetop
Pinecone, gaining speed,
Lands below – shattering silence.

We try to light the night
To continue the day.
Humans.

Love lights more than
Dawn or Day.
Love lights us from inside.

No matter how many candles
Grace your cake,
More light is always welcome.

A smile in the dark
Lightens the stormiest
Night.

Earth slumbers, restlessly
Rolling over,
Causing catastrophes.

Don't let Sleep
Trick you
Into thinking it is Nighttime.

Who speaks, who moves,
Who eats, who sees,
Step back inside – check.

In Presence
A flood of whitest Light
Reveals inner- and outer-scapes.

Day and night
Become a whole
In the timeless world.

Worlds in worlds,
From diatom to whale,
Life thrives.

Scale of what
You see, touch, hear,
Can limit and define your world.

Night creatures
Seem spooky to us,
Probably, much as we are to them.

Rain washes down the mountainside
Revealing new blades
In the weak October light.

Time to stoke fires
And knit woolen socks,
Winter seeks us out again.

Rocks poke out of the ground,
Earth bones,
Unashamed in full daylight.

Red earth under farmer's plough,
Potatoes rolling into view,
Slanting sunrays capturing harvest.

Etched in memory,
Scenes from childhood past,
Monuments to who we think we are.

Inner light
Brings introspection,
Without Presence, wasted.

Go deep inside,
Pull out old laundry,
Wash clean and air the lot.

Creatures gotta eat,
Feed what feeds You,
Starve the rest.

Long evenings,
Twilight twinkles,
Wine glasses clink.

Ground is thick with leaf offerings,
Red-gold blanket,
Whipped to frenzy in windy sunlight.

Light fades from my window,
My heart
Leaps to meet soft night of Love.

Always a surprise
First rays of Autumn sun,
Birds go crazy.

Cold light creeping beneath
My bedroom blinds,
Pokes at my eyelids.

At the end of your rope,
Take in
Flowering chrysanthemums.

Short is our stay,
Make way
With gusto.

Snowfall covers
All mistakes,
Be grateful.

Light on snow,
Like nothing
Ever imagined.

Long neon light stripes
Decorate
Newly mowed lawn.

Cloud strands stretch across
Winter's sky,
Pointing my way home.

Heart's journey:
Arduous and steep,
Love's climb to acceptance.

Be absolutely
Certain
Of only one thing.

A butterfly in a world on fire
Is naive,
But still, a butterfly.

Warm restless nights,
Burning hot days,
August lasts forever.

Who is really in charge,
When my feelings
Swirl around bars of my prison?

One snowflake
On old oak leaf,
White on brown in my hand.

Chess pieces diminish
One by one;
Fall by the wayside.

Win or lose
The checkered squares
Remain.

Taking risks, playing safe,
In the end –
Only a game.

Sadness follows my trailing
Vines,
From the shallows to the deeps.

Dark days,
Darker moods,
Twisting for the light.

So many stellar bodies
Pack the heavens
With their shining array.

The space between the stars
Looks small,
Maybe it is to them.

Outshined by Day,
Night must acquiesce,
And keep its subtleties.

Look how gradually
The light increases
With the volume of the birds.

Still your mind,
Lest your body
Have no peace.

A misstep can land us in trouble,
But drop sleep
From our eyes.

Pain, a signal,
Time to pay attention
To past evasions.

Lay a pathway of flowers
At the doorstep
Of the Beloved.

No Day or Night
In Heaven,
Only continuous divine Light.

Moon with her
Borrowed radiance,
Spotlights treacherous pathway.

Whispering about the scarlet Moon,
Pines shoulder together,
Blocking her light.

Night clutches her mysteries
Tightly
To her ebony breast.

Only dawn can unravel
The convoluted knots
Of deepest night.

From mountains to pebbles
Everything has its place
In Nature's garden.

Rain washes my eyes
And waters the roses
To perfection.

The quiet reflection
Of moonlight
Joins me on the terrace.

Be diligent
Such a short while
Roses bloom.

Bending to retrieve
Wayward blueberries
Intent on escape.

Lingering in the garden,
Dusk chases away
The last trace of color.

Spider's glistening web,
Unsuspecting end
For visiting fly.

Spring's allurements
Fade with Earth's journey,
A temporary glamor.

Dying embers
Of Summer's heat,
Blaze up in Autumn's raiment.

A child in us pleads, "Tell me a story
"How Winter met Spring,
"How Night met Dawn."

Love connects
And filters
Gold flecks.

Art communicates
Love between
Art form and recipient.

Sleeping leaders
Lead sleeping public
To their evaporated seabeds.

Lifesaving waters
Engulf parched throats
Diluting blood's heaviness.

Dull light shows
Empty garden
Since you left.

An arrow of
Wild geese
Point South once more.

Rains begin the endless
Stream of shrunken days
'Til frost covers all.

Long dark wait
For white cygnets'
Return.

First snow covers all,
But a pair of eyes
Mars perfect white.

Cactus has need
Of her spines,
Thirsty beings long for her store.

Late Summer's tired heat
Snakes along dry creek,
And chokes empty well.

Plodding steps,
Burning toes,
Closer to my shadow now.

Mirage looming, swallow hard,
Breathe deep, blow away illusion,
Pick up those feet.

Each day-season-year
Has its trials, its treasures,
Worthy of harvesting.

Love the difficulty
That teaches
Lessons of acceptance.

Green surrounding mountains,
White falls crashing on
Wet black rocks.

Blue depth
Seen through the well of air,
Confounds the limited mind.

Sky of light,
Sky of stars,
Sky shell of our world.

High puffy palaces,
Enormous white mounds,
Will turn dark and rain empty.

Lightning flashes blue-white
Harsh,
Stabs the ground with hot fingers.

Windy sea view,
White-topped waves,
Gull crested.

Sun-filled lavender field,
Framed by linden trees,
Bee's heaven.

Midnight blue star-studded velvet,
Cushions
Night's cold bumpy road.

Dark river trails
Throughout dusky meadow,
Tree roots gone wild.

Evening lights
Guide us to
Our celebration together.

If we were given Luck,
How would we use it?
Only well, if we were lucky.

Love all the questions
More than the answers,
There is only so much time.

The Whirling Dervish in my mind
Urges me
To reach beyond my thoughts.

Light opens the way
Through dark hallways
To more lucid perceptions.

Without the contrast
Of light and dark
Would we see anything?

Cross your fingers,
Toes, and everything else:
That luck brings you joy.

The hush
After the Sun sets,
Wiggles the hairs on my neck.

Graceful are the long-legged cranes,
Twice so
In the air.

Blankets up to my ears,
Cool seeping down the wall,
Spreading toward my toes.

Eyes and ears suddenly alert,
Strangeness bumping thumping
In the dark.

Ordinary in the day,
Transforms to
Extraordinary in the night.

Horse painted in patches
Rests in cool grass
Under old white oak.

Many black-faced sheep
Rub wool together,
Wary of nearby canines.

Descending light
Splashes pools of gray
Into every crevice.

Mournful loons
Announce approaching
Night.

Dressing for dinner,
Slicking fur,
Cat stalks her prey.

The disk of youngsters
Cycling the mother Sun,
Stay in their plane of order.

Glancing up
Stars overwhelmed me.
I drowned in their liquid fire.

Morning's heat
Coursed down the hillsides,
Soaked into the simmering valley.

We raise our hopes
To meet the Dawn
With renewed conviction.

Complicated
Usually means
Limited understanding.

Simple delights
Unlock states
And smiles.

Sweet cloud
Bathing my garden
With your precious gift.

How to repay
All that is given
Each day that we breathe?

A Sea of Dreams
Does not always foster
Nightmares.

On my porch
Double sphinx,
Guarding me from mice attack.

Clasped hands
Holding myself together,
In preparation for nightfall.

Self-raised state
Is not so common,
High alchemy.

Light in the light:
Indiscernible.
Light in the dark: brilliant.

Autumn breezes
Carry wood fire smoke,
Traces of savory barbecue.

Never-ending piles of dry leaves,
Joy,
For kids and dogs.

Black, white and gold
Dancing,
Moonlight rapture.

Meeting in daylight,
Joining others at dusk,
Celebrating at midnight.

Long awaited
Reunion,
At day's end.

He who loses
Joy,
Stands on barren ground.

Gravity well,
So easily slipped into,
Black hole of Night.

Alone,
The blaze of heaven
Has starred her vault.

Difficult to resist
Those flowers
On the mountainside.

The setting Sun
So oft
Showcases chosen pines.

My shadow before me,
Our star warms my back,
All the way home.

Call to Allah,
Day and Night,
Longing song.

Temples, minarets,
Steeples, towers,
Ever reaching for heaven.

Erect your worship house
Inside your
Soul.

Plumage in the sunlight
A good move
To attract would-be lovers.

Gray and empty
Garden,
'Til you return.

Love language
Needs no words
To share its tenderness.

My tongue
Frozen in my mouth,
Night screams muted.

Daybreak dispelling
Dark terrors,
Smoke rising.

Never alone,
But feeling so,
Veil of sadness descends.

Difficult to remember
The flowers of Spring,
When the last leaves fall.

Layers upon layers,
Life's debris,
Muddles thoughts.

Days and nights
Of growing wings,
Demands divided attention.

Mistakes, accidents, injuries,
Relentless heat,
August finally ending.

Long labor,
Little visible result,
Yet we continue.

Sunlight in the garden,
Tree framed,
Nose and eye feast.

Nestled in a bed of ruby leaves
Black dog wriggles
With joy.

Dew pearls,
Strung on spider's web,
Glisten wetly.

Would this moment
Still have happened,
Without my presence?

Daylight,
Open eye,
Brilliant!

Seemingly innocent,
Green-eye glint
Gives away all subterfuge.

Crickets suddenly stop,
What do they know?
That I don't.

Swim in the sea,
Toes in the sand,
Wind, waves, and You.

Beauty sees beauty,
We are what we
Long for.

Sappho must have loved her
Students.
Love flowed all the way to now.

Flowers,
Joined together
To bouquet.

Night jasmine
Starred the walk,
Mimicking Milky Way above.

We are so close,
Reality, truth, conscious existence,
If only we could let go of ourselves.

We must be grateful
For the slow and careful
Process of weaning us away.

Love's banquet:
A table set for all;
True blessing.

Neon-green rice fields
Shock the eye,
Hue of Spring in Fall.

Winging their journey South
Swans will be missed.
Empty fields without white feathers.

The rocks at the bottom
Of the hill –
Does anyone ever see them fall?

The only way to hang on to
This moment
Is to move with it.

Rainbow light,
Shattered white,
United in sequence.

Lake camouflaged in scenery
Hides its depths;
Wader's peril.

Green draining out of trees,
Wind pulling leaves from their perch.
Autumn gains momentum.

Many repeats overkill?
Our thick crust
Not easily penetrated.

Sleepy days
Makes for
Restless nights.

A fish in a bowl,
A bird in a cage,
My soul in this flesh.

From the blaze of Heaven,
To dark comfort of womb,
Landing in screaming cold light.

Home in endless light,
True self knows service
Through love.

Fruit of the Earth
Is the real fast food,
Undisturbed by packaging.

Animals eat to live without evil intent,
Makes civilized,
An odd choice to describe humans.

Piece by piece
I have left a trail
Of myself on this path.

He hunts
For the pesky loon
Hiding in the reedy lake.

Sweet twilight,
First stars
Peek over Black Mountain.

Moon hurtles
Herself across the pond,
Ripples with heroic abandon.

You cannot stop
The Sun and the Moon
From loving the Earth.

Accepting the Play
Does not mean
Giving up on your Self.

Small tastes
Tantalize.
Great gobs numb senses.

Curbing appetite
Intensifies
Satisfaction.

Instructions for living
Are not provided
At birth.

If you must seek,
Start with
Who you think you are.

Love every opportunity
To give
All you can.

The boomerang
Of Karma
Never ceases.

Light fading,
Below the window sill,
Candle glow brightens.

At the end of time,
Who remains
To lock doors and put out lights?

He who trusts,
Is trustworthy.
Aiming is halfway there.

The great circle of
Nothing,
Contains everything.

Never
Underrate
Stillness.

Am I satisfied
With partial awakening?
Do I long for completion?

Questions fairly asked,
Can lead
To awareness of the moment.

Light opens periphery,
Expands
Horizons.

Night comes upon us
Regularly,
Inhalation of Earth.

Beauty isn't necessary
Unless,
You want to live.

Water lilies,
Dragonflies,
Quiet pond.

What comes from the well
Disturbs
The gentle rest of sleepers.

Expectations are a setup
For a fall
To solid truth.

The need to harness life
Does not end well;
Being is life, unharnessed.

Air, earth, water, fire;
All can be life-giving,
Or vicious.

In the dark,
Touch and hearing
Become significant.

Distance is an
Aspect
Of daylight.

Over the night,
Woes and ills
Can be cleansed.

A new day,
A new Sun,
Another chance.

Drop all pretenses
That this you,
Is all You are.

Overwhelmed with the sight,
Autumn color
Provokes a breathy, "Oooooh."

The mountain lifts its beauty up
Through the trees
Visible, proud, majestic.

Ignite your inner fire
However you can,
Shared flame works well.

Same as using the right tool,
Using the right energy
Will accomplish the aim.

Late Summer Sun,
Late afternoon rose gold light,
Not too late to enjoy.

Moving low in the sky
Sun bows to grand entrance:
Queen of Night rises.

Night walking,
Moon shadow for company
On star jasmine path.

Blackberry bushes,
Empty of their delicious fruit,
Scratching legs and boots.

Pumpkin goldenness
Filling the patch,
Watermelons only memory.

Crows perched
On scarecrow's shoulders,
Irony illustrated.

Crowding marigolds drawing
Butterflies,
Bees.

Tentative light
Feeling the night's ending,
Streaks forth in pink and white.

Sensitive to beginnings
And endings,
We tread carefully.

Unburdened tree branch,
Free to wave
In the cold wind.

In full daylight
Smallest detail
Can be seen.

Deepest night
Of darkest cave,
Still home to bats.

Small beings
Have a bit
Of mind and heart.

Dividing up the god pie,
A tiny slice goes to
Every creature.

A million heartbeats
Allotted to each
Lifetime of moments.

So graced,
Days of light,
Nights of quiet peace.

Here,
In this now,
I am.

Naked, alive,
Mostly whole,
Looking around my world.

Six days lead to
Unlimited daylight
Forever.

Starry night, deep rest,
Moon as reflection
Of day to return.

We divide, separate,
To determine, understand,
Sometimes forgetting wholeness.

Hours, days, nights, weeks, months,
How much time
Makes Presence?

Awake in day,
Awake in night,
Awake timeless.

Celebrate another year
Free
Of tormenting imagination.

Looking up,
The wonder of the stars
Still thrills.

Sunlight on water,
A reflection almost unbearable
For our gentle eyes.

Love is beyond
Sight, sound, touch,
Love transcends life.

Hot and parched,
Water of life,
Great need of you.

On my way to meet You,
Noticing
You were already here.

Both light and dark
Are inside my head,
Telling their stories.

Thank you for 46 years
Of connection
To a truer Self.

Remember to feed what you love,
Starve
What does not love You.

Great passions
Suit novels,
Try to have relativity.

September,
Month of transition,
Slowly losing light.

A friend told me,
Remember:
Each step you take is critical.

Wind whispers
Chiding sunburnt fields,
Hinting at coming frost.

We care,
Sometimes too much,
Broken hearts mend eventually.

Grave day,
Pleasant hour,
Happy moment.

For those who leave us,
And don't look back,
We salute you on your journey home.

Heart strands
Clipped short,
Sting and clamor for connection.

Sometimes
"All is perfect"
Is an imperfect achievement.

We acknowledge
The greatest among us,
By seeking their company.

Snowflake melts
At body temperature,
Like frozen illusions.

Greet each morning
With refreshed aims,
For renewed presence.

Dancing at the ball,
Cinderella
Reveals her true face.

Presence acquired
Is momentous,
Unbidden – a priceless gift.

Cupid sends love particles
Riding on light waves,
Be careful of sunburn.

Follow the petals
To the center
Of the rose.

Scorched ground
Craving splash of rain,
To save small forest beings.

Awareness in a world of sleep
Would be lonely,
Except for angels.

Aromatic flowers
Brighten
A gloomy atmosphere.

Days pile up,
Then are suddenly
Gone.

Empty your wallet,
Pay all your attention,
To what is really important.

A new life
Is precious,
Unless it's a bug.

A hall of classic paintings
Cannot compare to the beauty
Of one fresh flower.

All creation
Is imitation
Of original existence.

Strange sounds and sights
In the dark of night,
Become a refrigerator in daytime.

Sky and lake
Meet at
Double sunset.

Beauty doesn't wait
For our appreciation,
It is up to us to enjoy.

The demands of life
Can overshadow
The need for real living.

The sphere of discipline
Sits atop
The cube of infinity.

Days of endless light,
Alternate
With finite dark nights.

Earth makes her own
Shadow,
Turned from father's shining face.

The eye of each
Yin and Yang:
Kernel of the other half.

Best not forget the light
Or the dark,
When being in either.

Particles of God
Are synonymous with
Particles.

Even with infinite light,
Camera of our eye
Sees nothing without photographer.

Gifts for friends afar
Carried by more friends;
Love traveling across ocean.

Full Sun,
Enormous glare,
Heat heavier than lead.

Earth is no closer to our star,
Yet increased temperature;
Mystery incandescence.

Palm trees, colorful umbrellas,
White tablecloths,
We gather to cheer each other.

Difficult to be
Gracious
In meltdown mode.

Moving through space,
Hair streaming behind,
Bicycle humming.

Morning repast, coffee,
Many voices,
Heat rising.

Deer family outside my door
Looking askance,
Very thirsty.

Autumn spreads her skirts,
And covers dry ground
With beautiful mosaic patterns.

Heat waves shimmering
Over flat fields
Baking last of green clover.

Nights of heat
Steamy, smokeless,
Blanket-less.

Cat and mouse
Alike
Are hot tonight.

We struggle to survive,
But not as humbly
As what struggles with us.

Health is overlooked
By youth,
Revered by the aged.

Like the Moon
I'm in tidal lock,
With Your face.

Love is ageless,
Timeless,
Beyond life and death.

Trip across the ocean,
Visit with loving friends;
Memories engraved.

Earth undressing,
Overheated,
Even oceans too warm.

Cooler nights rest weary
Sun-stroked land,
Brief interludes between bakings.

Extra pressure –
Cosmic influences
Pull and push all the buttons.

The sacred space between
Your brows
Knows the truth in your heart.

Light created by Sun is necessary,
But can't compare
With light uncreated.

The darkness inside our bodies
Is pierced by light
In unusual ways.

Rhythms of day and night
Comprise our lives
In a long drumbeat dance.

Purpose, deliberation,
Imply a designer;
Someone to blame or praise.

It is best to take responsibility:
Fault or credit
Can be assigned later.

Scenery changes with light,
But not as much as with the viewer;
Subjectivity is a facet of humanity.

Questions abound,
But none so profound,
As, "To be or not to be."

Those who have gone before us,
Leave traces which we can use,
If we open our minds and hearts.

Anniversary of one's birth,
Another trip around our star,
70 years on planet Earth.

Dance in the day,
Dance in the night,
But, by all means, dance!

The clouds part,
Beholding the harvest Moon,
Deeply satisfying.

Frost-tipped leaf piles,
Shortened daylight,
Winter announcing approach.

Love glistens on wet tree trunks,
Sparkling in puddles,
And streaming on cliff side.

Old friends
With good hearts,
Are grateful to be present together.

How can we pray for things,
When we have been given
Everything.

Patience bears all,
With good will
And grace.

Time is a commodity,
Spend carefully and
Respectfully.

To be among the few,
Requires personal commitment,
As well as personal payment.

We are visions for each other,
Wonderful friends,
So much happiness here.

Celebrations are events,
Worthy of capturing
In our memories.

Here, in this now,
Spread good cheer,
Be your real Self.

In the stillness,
Let your beating heart,
Touch your soul.

Patches of Summer blue
Between the waving tree branches,
Welcome me home.

Anticipation is a form
Of imagination,
Difficult to resist.

Did Beethoven really
Experience
All those emotions?

We are so very lucky
To have such a variety of
Beautiful music.

Voices can be like
Silk or gravel;
It is a good way to assess state.

Even in movement
Inner stillness
Encourages Presence.

Little shocks wait for us
Everywhere we look,
Especially where we don't.

Threadbare and worn,
Repeatedly rereading
My copy of Zen living.

Bolstering courage,
Stepping forward,
From the dark into the light.

Those unturned rocks
Can haunt our moments,
In the search for true Self.

Sometimes payment comes first,
And after,
The blessed event.

Family is a tradition
That outlives
Many cultural changes.

Friend connections
Are like a safety net,
Of sincere affection.

We help each other
As we have been helped,
Enormously, on this path.

Remains of the day
Loom large,
As night falls.

Each moment
Is perfect unto itself,
And fits exactly into the whole.

To be beautiful
Is to hold beauty,
In your heart.

Avoiding the unpleasant,
Makes significant,
That which isn't.

Our plans
Fall short
Of the grand design.

Languid days
Can foster
Sleepless nights.

Labor is fraught
With subjective opinions,
Real work is for high purposes.

Interesting how season change
Can make our whole world,
Feel changed.

We are such stuff
That pervades
The universe.

Outside our planet
Zen days and nights
Are one and the same.

We take our atmosphere
For granted,
Until smoke defiles it.

A clean breeze
Becomes a priceless
Gift.

Love is contagious
Fortunately,
Circulating faster than air.

Finding an incredible key
Is almost as good as
Finding the way to use it.

Across the night sky,
A meteor streams,
Leaving its fiery tail behind.

Omens are harbingers
Of coming changes,
Presence rides the waves.

The strength of daylight,
Hides outer space activity
From our limited view.

One less queen,
One new king,
Roles reassigned.

Angels in our lives
Disallowing too much sleep,
Love embodied, love extended.

We may not always be able
To show our gratitude;
Deep within us lives acceptance.

Strewn across the lawn
Forgotten pine needles,
Make soft bed for white kitten.

Being deeply loved
Enables us to love,
A current of divine destiny.

Smoke-filled red sunlight
A little scary,
Air almost unbreathable.

Ushers coming tonight,
Friends rejoined,
Harmony sustained.

Ninth month of the year
Slipping into Fall,
Vibrant trees paving the way.

There is no balance for Day
Without the counterpoint
Of Night.

Harmony of the spinning
Planets
Creates unearthly music.

To hear the beating heart
Of the universe
Cosmic hearing is required.

Many hands lessen toil,
Many hearts strengthen
Love effort.

Books are for the quiet-minded,
Singular,
Simple and personal.

We are moving in the same
Direction,
Regardless of motive.

We spin
With the Earth,
Whether we want to or not.

Love is the mover,
The changer, the canceller,
Love is, and does, everything.

Roses fill the air
With heady perfume,
Ephemeral invisible beauty.

I purloined one of your
Godiva chocolates;
You graciously forgave me.

Everything changes,
Movement is life,
Presence is eternal.

The life of one person
Is unique and commonplace,
Simultaneously.

With presence,
Existence becomes
Immortality.

Our dark and our light side,
Our sleep and our presence,
Are necessary for evolution.

How can it be
That there are so many stars,
Beyond counting?

We have a place to live on Earth
For now;
We adapt to most things.

Blessings beyond measure
Have showered us daily,
We barely comprehend.

Beautiful woman
Shining above the ancient pond,
Grace to grace bestowed.

Earth's seasons help us
To understand
Cycles in our own lives.

Lacy leaf patterns
Against deep blue patches;
Luscious sky quilt.

Trail your fingers through
Leaf-strewn pond,
Watch for small fish bites.

Blue heron watches silently
For small fish
Rising to surface.

Nature foments
All manifestations,
Spirit draws us higher.

Red maple leaves
Igniting clouds
Over setting Sun.

Lone pine
Silhouetted
Atop dark hill.

Singular thought
In Solitude;
Complete stillness.

Night framing
Candle glow,
Contemplating truth.

Glasses of ruby wine,
Sweet friends
Sharing tender moments.

Nothing stirs,
Silent stillness,
An unnatural morning.

Great groans
Erupting from
Ancient cat on the move.

Piles of deep purple grapes,
Harvest well on the way
To fill the barrels.

Shivering tiny hairs
Along my arms,
Whenever You appear.

The inner eye
Sees from
The heart.

To love
As we are loved,
Is an ongoing challenge.

Movement of time
Through sky changes:
Dawn, Day, Dusk, Night.

I would paint Your portrait,
If my brush could be the air
And my palette the dawn.

Fill your senses
With early morning delights,
Day's promise begins with a kiss.

Dig deep into
Night's hidden secrets,
Arise with renewed conviction.

Fathoms below the surface,
At the bottom of the ocean
Lies the source of suppressed fears.

Ant climbs over yellow roses
Searching for
Breakfast crumbs.

Mountain lions, poison oak,
Rattlesnakes, bears,
Country living has its hazards.

If dying is lucky,
We are guaranteed
One hundred percent luck.

It's an illusion
To think that Presence
Is an option.

A drop shoots up
The circle left in the pond,
By the leaping frog.

Rice on the floor,
Pots bubbling over,
She is cooking, again.

In the deepest woods
A single chestnut tree
Flirts with the dusk breezes.

The empty part of night
Contains my whole
Tomorrow.

Who taught you
To be you?
Who are you, now?

A bird landed on my windowsill,
Does he see himself,
Or is he really looking at me?

Our lives and plans continue…
Do we attend to the play of
Small moments?

Shorter days, longer nights,
To meet eternity
Stretch out elastic moments.

After last breath,
Free of heavy Earth,
Will I appreciate the dawn?

Thrills are short-lived,
Personally invigorating,
Objectively nonexistent.

Tell a story to a child,
But not
To your wife.

Great is the whole of creation,
Small is our space within it,
And not in the center.

Discarded leaves brown and curled,
Swirl up behind me,
As I run.

Gray days and nights seem empty,
Longing piles them
Like leaves for bonfire.

Beauty exists even without a viewer,
Residing in remote places.
Gather up as much as you can.

We ascend together,
Pearls sewn on the garment
Of the rising angel.

Zen days, smooth and even,
Zen nights, black satin rest,
Zen life, realized.

Discord, grumpy bumpy road,
Transformed;
A new jewel in the crown.

Waking to gratitude,
Tears pool around
Broken illusions.

One moment times a thousand
Cannot give presence,
You bestow the greatest gift.

Our extended family
Shares highs and lows.
We carry each other forward.

A Teacher's generosity
Makes love possible,
Guiding us to the ultimate light.

Leap over obstacles,
Not everything needs confrontation,
Let all unnecessary fade away.

Zen jewels
Sparkle in day,
Becoming glowing embers at night.

Forgetting happens,
Following the clues back to one's Self,
Compulsory.

Always begin,
Therein lies
The secret answer.

Zen days seep into
Zen nights,
Especially with no eyes.